To

_____

From

_____

Date

_____

My Rhyme-Time Bible
for little ones

Donna Clark Goodrich

HARVEST HOUSE PUBLISHERS
EUGENE, OREGON

Jesus said, "Let the little children come to me
and do not try to stop them,
for the kingdom of heaven belongs to such as these."

Matthew 19:14

My Rhyme-Time Bible for little ones

Text Copyright © 2016 by Donna Clark Goodrich
Artwork Copyright © 2016 by Harvest House Publishers

Published by Harvest House Publishers
Eugene, Oregon 97402
www.harvesthousepublishers.com

978-0-7369-5549-2

Printed in China

15 16 17 18 19 20 21 22 23 24 / DS-NPP / 10 9 8 7 6 5 4 3 2 1

Who and What

God's Fun Week

So very many years ago,
God made the land and seas.
Then He made the bright blue sky,
The flowers, and the trees.

He set the golden sun up high
To give us warmth and light,
The silver moon, the twinkling stars
To light the sky at night.

He made the birds that soar so high
With many colored feathers.
He placed the fish down in the sea
To swim there all together.

Then He made the animals—
Giraffes that stand so tall,
Cows and horses, sheep and pigs,
And puppies soft and small.

Last, God said, "I'll make man
To love and worship Me.
And I'll give him a wife
To keep him company."

Aren't you glad God made
This world bright and new?
And aren't you thankful
That He created YOU?

What is your favorite
animal that God created?

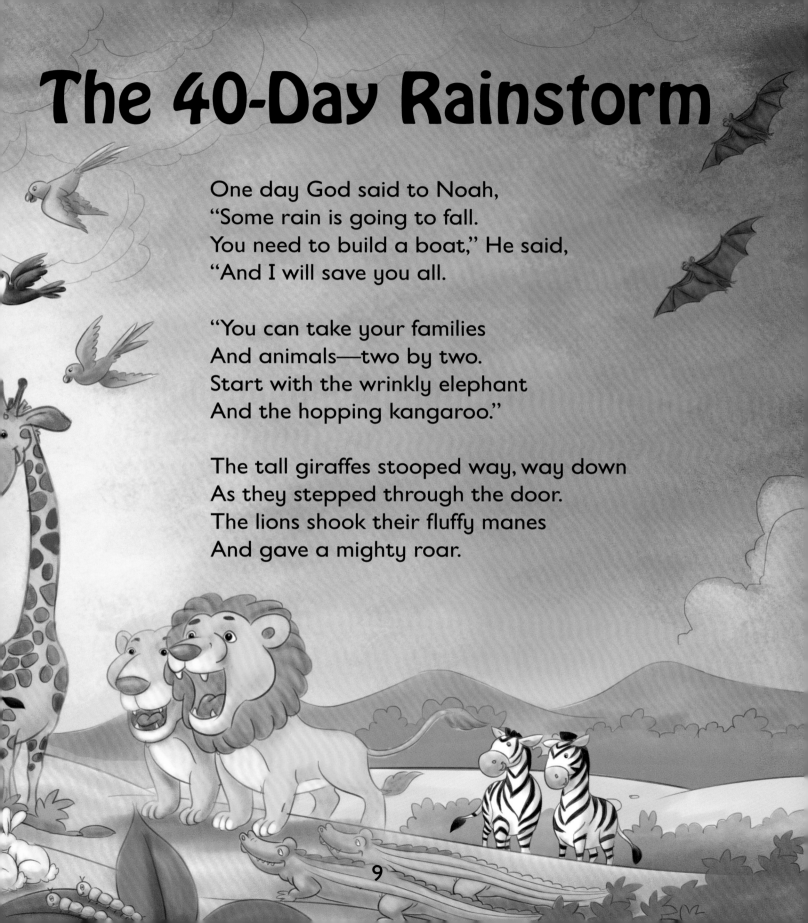

The 40-Day Rainstorm

One day God said to Noah,
"Some rain is going to fall.
You need to build a boat," He said,
"And I will save you all.

"You can take your families
And animals—two by two.
Start with the wrinkly elephant
And the hopping kangaroo."

The tall giraffes stooped way, way down
As they stepped through the door.
The lions shook their fluffy manes
And gave a mighty roar.

The monkeys hurried to the boat,
Not wanting to be late.
The peacocks spread their feathers
And said, "Don't we look great?"

After 40 days and nights of rain,
The land began to dry.
When Noah left the ark, he saw
A rainbow in the sky.

If there are times you are afraid
And don't know what to do,
Remember God saved Noah,
And He'll protect you too.

What would you do if it rained for 40 days
and you couldn't go outside to play?

Abraham
Faithful Man of God

There was a man named Abraham,
And Sarah was his wife.
They were sad because they had
No children in their life.

Abraham was a godly man—
Prayed to the Lord each day.
He heard God say that they must move
To a new land far away.

So Abraham took his wife,
His cattle, and his sheep
And journeyed up the river
To a mountain tall and steep.

13

One day God said to Abraham,
"See those stars up in the sky?
That's how many children that
You'll have before you die."

God did not forget His word.
The glad day finally came
When Sarah had a little boy,
And Isaac was his name.

Whenever you think of this tale,
There's one thing you should know:
God promised that He'll be with you
Wherever you may go.

Have you ever had to move?
Did you like it?
Why or why not?

Joseph
From Pit to Palace

Joseph was his father's favorite.
And much to his surprise,
He was given a many-colored coat.
He could not believe his eyes.

This made his brothers angry.
They nearly had a fit.
So they ripped off Joseph's coat
And threw him in a pit.

Joseph knew that God was with him,
So he didn't fear a thing.
He ended up in Egypt
In the palace of the king.

A famine lasted seven years.
There was no food or rain.
People came from all around,
And Joseph gave them grain.

The brothers came to ask for some,
But little did they know
That Joseph was the brother
They had mistreated so.

When Joseph told them who he was,
They feared what he would say.
But he said that he forgave them,
That God had led the way.

When you do something wrong, tell your mom or
dad you're sorry. Tell Jesus too, and He'll forgive you.

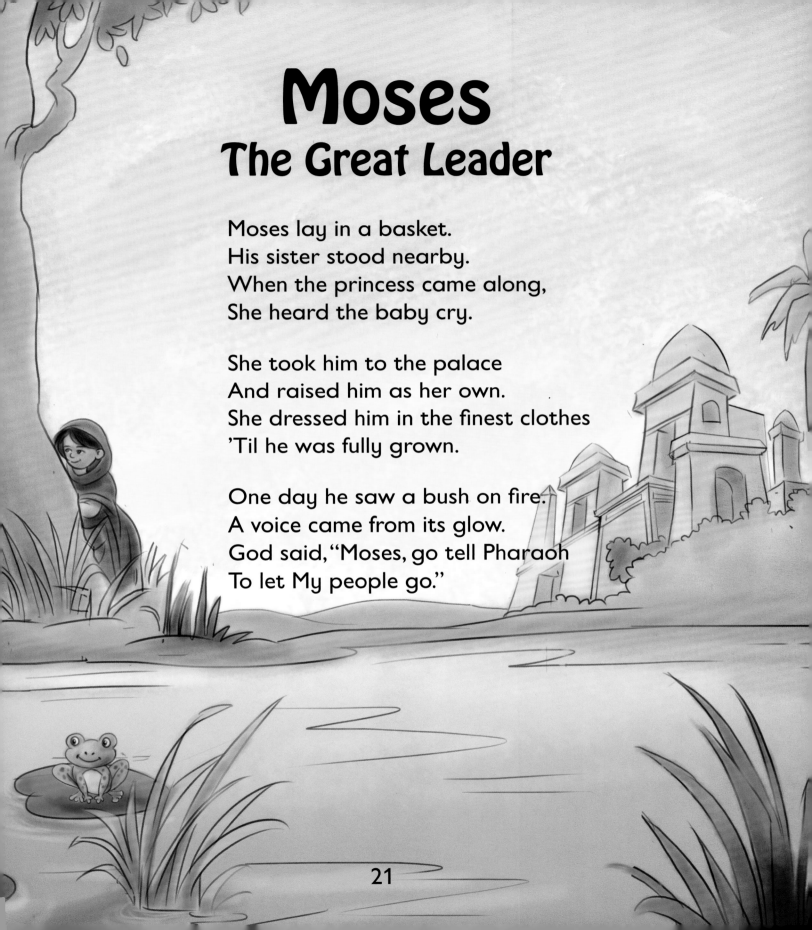

Moses
The Great Leader

Moses lay in a basket.
His sister stood nearby.
When the princess came along,
She heard the baby cry.

She took him to the palace
And raised him as her own.
She dressed him in the finest clothes
'Til he was fully grown.

One day he saw a bush on fire.
A voice came from its glow.
God said, "Moses, go tell Pharaoh
To let My people go."

The evil Pharaoh finally said
He'd set God's people free.
But then he sent his soldiers
To stop them at the sea.

They asked, "How will we get across?
The river is so wide."
But God split the Red Sea open,
And they marched to the other side.

God called Moses once again
To climb up on a mountain.
God gave him the Ten Commandments.
Let's see if you can count them:
1   2   3   4   5   6   7   8   9   10

One of the Commandments says
to honor your dad and mom.
This means to do what they ask
you to do. How can you honor
your dad or mom today?

Ruth
Loyal to Her Family

Naomi sadly lost her sons
And prepared to move away.
She asked their wives if they would like
To go with her or stay.

The one named Orpah said to her,
"I'm staying here, I know."
But the other one named Ruth replied,
"Where you go, I will go."

Their new life was very hard,
But Ruth did not complain.
Each day she worked the fields
To gather up the grain.

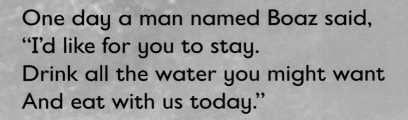

One day a man named Boaz said,
"I'd like for you to stay.
Drink all the water you might want
And eat with us today."

Then Ruth and Boaz fell in love.
Their wedding day soon came.
Later on they had a son,
And Obed was his name.

Ruth loved and trusted God,
Who was with her all the way,
And if you love Him, He will be
With you through every day.

Ruth was one of Jesus' ancestors, which means family who lived a long time ago. How many of your family members can you name?

Samuel
Answers God's Call

Hannah longed to have a child
And knew what she must do.
"If You give me a son," she prayed,
"I'll give him back to You."

God heard Hannah's prayer that day
And filled her heart with joy.
Before the year was over,
God gave her a little boy.

Hannah named this child Samuel,
And this mother kept her word.
She took him to the temple
So he could serve the Lord.

One night while Samuel was in bed,
He heard his name three times.
He did not know the voice that called,
So out of bed he climbed.

But Eli, knowing it was God,
Told Samuel what to do.
"The next time just say, 'Lord, it's me.
I'm listening to You.'"

God used Samuel as a preacher,
And He can use you too.
Even though you may be small,
He has work for you to do.

What are some things you can do today
to show your love for Jesus?

David
and the Big Guy

David was a shepherd boy
Who watched sheep as they lay.
And while he watched, he liked to sing
And play his harp all day.

One day he fixed a basket lunch
And took it to his brothers.
And then he saw a great **BIG** man
Who was scaring all the others.

Goliath was the giant's name.
"Come out and fight," he cried.
But all the soldiers shook with fear.
They wanted to run and hide.

33

David said, "The Lord saved me
From a lion and a bear."
And with his sling, he shot a stone.
It sailed right through the air.

Smack! It hit Goliath's head,
And he tumbled to the ground.
The rest of his army ran away.
They were nowhere to be found.

There may be times when you're afraid,
But God will help you too.
Simply pray, "Please be with me
And help me live for You."

What are you afraid of? Have you asked Jesus to take away your fear? He'll do it.

Daniel
In the Lions' Den

Daniel was a young man
Who wanted to do what's right.
He prayed to God three times a day
And often prayed at night.

Some evil men went to the king
And said, "Please let it be
That people pray to only you."
To this the king agreed.

The king then signed a paper,
Which said that all the men
Who prayed to any but the king
Go in the lions' den.

But Daniel kept on praying
With his window open wide.
He wasn't scared because he knew
The Lord was on his side.

They threw poor Daniel in the den,
But God had heard his call.
Snap! He shut the lions' mouths.
Daniel escaped them all!

If ever you're in trouble
And don't know what to do,
Just say a prayer to Daniel's God,
And He will help you too.

Have you ever seen a lion at a zoo or on TV?
Why wasn't Daniel afraid?

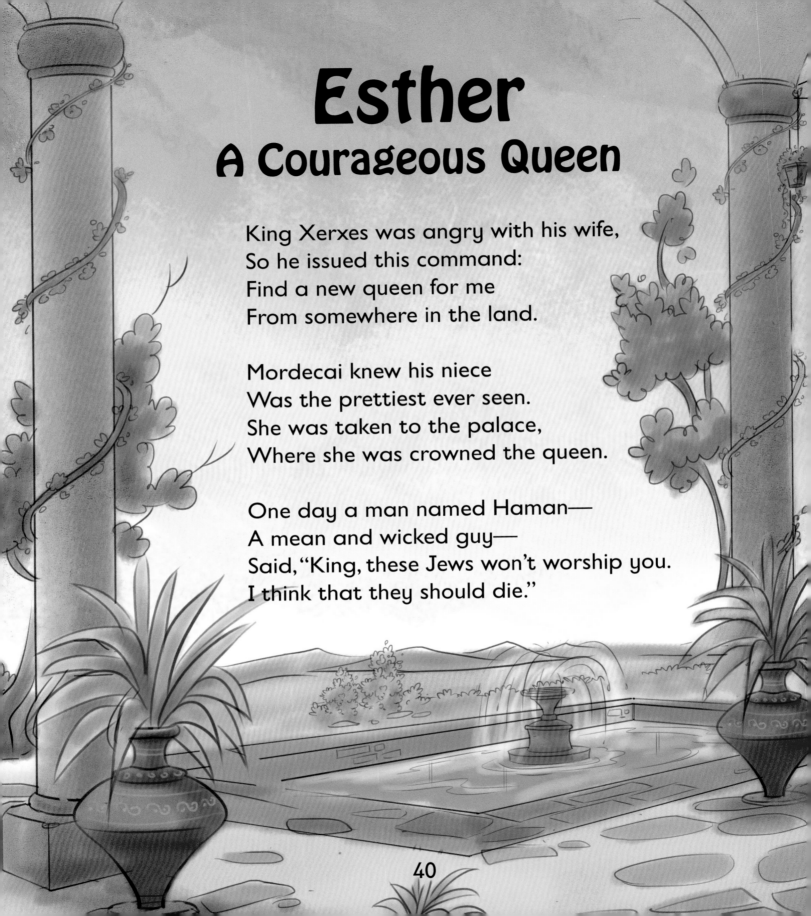

Esther
A Courageous Queen

King Xerxes was angry with his wife,
So he issued this command:
Find a new queen for me
From somewhere in the land.

Mordecai knew his niece
Was the prettiest ever seen.
She was taken to the palace,
Where she was crowned the queen.

One day a man named Haman—
A mean and wicked guy—
Said, "King, these Jews won't worship you.
I think that they should die."

40

"Go to the king and hurry!"
Mordecai told the queen.
"Tell him Haman's plan is evil
And that he is very mean."

Esther asked Haman and the king
To a meal she made one day.
"O King, my people will be killed.
Do something right away."

Haman then was punished,
And God's people all were saved.
Because Esther trusted God,
He helped her to be brave.

Repeat this verse: "I will trust and not be afraid."
Thank God for being with you at all times.

A New Baby
in Bethlehem

Joseph took Mary to Bethlehem.
They had no place to sleep
Until an innkeeper led them to
A stable with cows and sheep.

Then as the moon shone overhead
In the very early morn,
A cry came from the stable
As a little Boy was born.

When shepherds saw an angel,
They didn't know what to do.
But the angel said, "Don't be afraid.
I bring good news to you."

The shepherds listened closely
As the angel spoke this word:
"A special Babe is born tonight—
A Savior, Christ the Lord."

The angels left and the shepherds said,
"Let's go see this little stranger."
They went to Bethlehem and found
The Baby in a manger.

As Jesus grew to boyhood,
He loved to run and play.
The Bible tells us that He grew
In wisdom every day.

Jesus was a child just like you. He helped His father in the
carpenter's shop. What can you do today to help your parents?

Jesus
the Miracle Worker

When Jesus walked upon this earth,
He healed the sick and poor.
We call these healings *miracles*.
Would you like to hear some more?

A friend named Lazarus had been in
A tomb for four long days.
Jesus raised him from the dead
While all around gave praise.

When sailing on the stormy seas,
The disciples grew afraid.
"Peace! Be still," Christ spoke aloud.
To that the waves obeyed.

Two blind men came to Jesus.
"Please heal us!" they both cried.
"Do you believe?" He asked the two.
And their eyes were opened wide.

One day a crowd of thousands
Needed to be fed.
They all were served with just two fish
And five small loaves of bread.

Jesus still does miracles,
And you can have a part.
Say, "I'm sorry for my sins.
Please come into my heart."

Thank Jesus for making you and for everything He has given you. What are some of these things?

The Lost Son Comes Home

A man in the Bible had two sons,
And the youngest said one day,
"I want my share of money, Dad.
I'm going to go away."

Soon he spent his money
And didn't know what to do.
He had to work among the pigs,
Eating with them too.

One day he stopped and wondered
What he was doing there?
While all his father's servants
Had food enough to spare.

He said to himself, "I'm going home,"
And then picked up his load.
His father saw him from afar
And came running down the road.

He threw his arms around his neck.
"I forgive you, son," he said.
"I'm so glad you're now home safe.
I thought that you were dead."

The servants brought new robes for him
And shoes to fit his feet.
They then prepared a feast for him,
And they all sat down to eat.

Have you ever had to tell your mother or
father that you're sorry for doing something?
Didn't it feel good when they forgave you?

Special Friends of Jesus

Jesus had 12 followers
Who were His special friends.
He called them His disciples
And He loved them to the end.

Among them were some fishermen,
Peter, James, and John.
They were the ones who heard God say,
"This is My beloved Son."

Jesus loved His cousin John
the Baptist, brave and true.
He baptized those who turned to God
And baptized Jesus too.

Of all the friends who Jesus had,
There were none He held so dear
As the little children who would come
To Him from far and near.

His disciples told them to go away,
But He told them, "Come to Me."
He laughed with them and talked with them
And held them on His knee.

Jesus still loves everyone—
Whether you are big or small—
But just like He did back then,
He loves children most of all.

Can you name some of your special friends?
Is Jesus one of them?

Peter
From Fisherman to Preacher

Peter was a fisherman,
But he left the life he'd planned
To follow Jesus where He led
As He taught throughout the land.

Yet fearing for his life one night,
Before the cock crowed thrice,
With enemies all around, he said
That he did not know Christ.

He felt so sad that he'd betrayed
The one he held so dear,
But Christ's love was with him still.
His forgiveness brought him cheer.

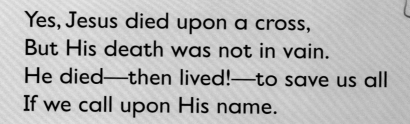

Yes, Jesus died upon a cross,
But His death was not in vain.
He died—then lived!—to save us all
If we call upon His name.

Though Christ was now in heaven above,
The story was not done,
For Peter had so much to do,
His work had just begun.

Peter spent his last days preaching
That Jesus rose up from the grave.
And to all who ask forgiveness,
He still has the power to save!

Jesus still is calling people to follow Him.
Just like He called Peter, He's calling you too!

Prayer

God, I may be very small,
But there's lots that I can do
To help my mom and daddy
And show my love for You.

I want to live for Jesus
And be His special friend.
Please come into my heart today,
In Jesus' name, amen.